Inappropriate Sleepover

Inappropriate Sleepover

meg johnson

The National Poetry Review Press
Aptos, California

The National Poetry Review Press
(an imprint of DHP)
Post Office Box 2080, Aptos, California 95001-2080

Inappropriate Sleepover
Copyright © 2014 Meg Johnson

Printed in the United States of America
Published in 2014 by The National Poetry Review Press

ISBN 978-1-935716-34-1

Cover artwork:

Bowery Bed
by Leslie Graff
mixed media on canvas, 11" x 14"
www.lesliegraff.com

for my mom, my dad, and my brother

Table of Contents

I'm a Victorian cowgirl with a clicking jaw.
I don't wear sweatpants with the word
TROUBLE printed on the ass because that
would be redundant. This is where I up the
ante by writing something even more offensive
like *I'm so hot I could impregnate myself*.
Somehow, even without the TROUBLE
sweatpants, there are people who yell "Trouble!"
at me from across the street. Sometimes people
yell "Timber!" but that's only when tall shoes
and margaritas are involved. If I was a tree I'd
want to be a pine because of the needles. People
would always be finding a piece of me. After
Christmas in the carpet, on a sweatshirt after a
long walk in the woods. Imagine the mind control!
That's really what it's about, right? To be the dog
that pees on everything that can never be
      forgotten, right?

The Girl

*"Girl, I can see you from a disss...tance...
Baby. I'd get run over by a car for you."*
-A man across the street
(Akron, Ohio)

I'm the girl with rocks
in her ballet flats. It doesn't
matter what city I move to.
I walk while men shout.
Rocks in my shoes.

But only in Akron, Ohio
am I mistaken for a prostitute.
I wear cardigans and knee
length skirts. Some men
don't assume I'm a prostitute
but try to talk me into it.
I keep walking by in my
Ann Taylor outfits.

The mattress store in my
neighborhood says CASH
TALKS   LOUD. I'm startled
when a plastic bag behind me
rustles in the wind. I'm floating
through cities. Internally groaning
at English professors who have
bands, but I smile politely because

they seem so gentle. They make
stray cats look like robbers. When I
see a stray cat, I cross the street.

Fascinatin' Rhythm

Somewhere between the moving
pianos, I could swear that I, myself,
was Eleanor Powell. In Wisconsin,
when you call for a cab, it often
arrives in the form of a minivan, the
vehicle ideal for transporting large
groups of college football fans. The
van will toss you around, and on your
way to the doctor, you'll realize you're
far from grounded. There are floating
pianos, but no scratchy taps and
certainly no lady-worn suits.

Before my first lesson
I saw a girl cry. I was
dropped off early.
The piano room had a curtain
for a door. I watched the end
of the other girl's lesson.
Not much older than I,
the girl seated at the piano
played and cried. The music
was totally indifferent.

"Be Prepared"

I quit Girl Scouts
the day after the troop
had polishing silver day.
It was a child's version
of buyer's remorse. It was like
you get married and your
spouse starts making pet
jewelry. Polishing silver was
a preview to dater's remorse.
I was 24 and on a third date.
My date's living room
was equipped with a
stripper pole and disco
ball. Like a sort of sexual
hostage, he forced a
strip tease-pole dance on me.
Scattered clothes around
the room. Him, upside down,
hanging from the pole.
Me, on the couch, like a
1950s secretary with
agoraphobia. Insides
like the desert.

A Green Dress

I thought a poem I wrote about sex
would be an amazing poem
because it was a poem about amazing sex
but when I looked out to the faces of my listeners
I could see their queasy expressions.
At that moment I realized my poem was
more porn than piece of art
which was a shame because I was
wearing a lovely green dress
to compliment my brown-black hair.
I have to say I looked amazing so at least
something was
amazing but my poem was not so I
went home to pout and called Elizabeth
who is my friend slash personal assistant.
I told Elizabeth to come over with a cheeseburger
for me and fries of course
and make it snappy.
To pass the time I jumped up and down
then I was tired and flopped on my bed.
Still waiting, I could already taste
her gratitude when I thanked her.

I Should Be in Jail

I wish I were in jail
because then I would be given
three free meals a day
and time to read
the books I really want
to read and time
to get really buff.
No one would pressure me to
renew an apartment lease
eleven months in advance.
I have no qualms about
the uniform. My high school
colors were orange and black,
which I rocked, especially as a
baton twirler. I've always
been complimented on my
license and ID photos so
pulling off a good mug shot
would be a snap. I've also been
wondering if I should have
experimented with being
a lesbian by now and prison
would give me plenty of time
to explore whether I'm bisexual.

Anyway, I just thought
I'd let you know what's new with
me now that we're dating again.
You can pretend to be turned off
by the idea of conjugal visits,
but you won't be fooling anyone.
I'm sure you could help me
find a good crime to commit.

The Unfortunate Charisma

it's like a locket but also
like Penny's computer book from Inspector Gadget
(under tights, under lace...)

it's like a pre-adolescent wearing tight jeans saying *I'm
a Samantha*

it's like missing a credit card payment

　　　　fists for ovaries

I'll admit I've been swayed by a sparkling spoon

it's...

watching a friend being taken away in a car
giddily he waves to you from the passenger seat;
you stand on the corner, the driver not offering you a ride

　　　　the name of my imaginary band is Kill The Colony

it's like a pregnancy dream with
　　　　no　　　　men

like an *oh-no-she-deh-ent* letter to the editor
strangers wave, they say *great letter*

my father as a young boy carves
Born To Be Wild in the boards
of the corn crib

he didn't have to tell me this
I can feel my DNA like a razor

Betty Boop Goes Goth

Sophomore year was an absolute
disaster for Betty. Being named second
runner-up at Miss Ohio Teen was
the low point. When David, the boy
from her biology class who wears makeup, said
she would make a good Goth girl
Betty lethargically said okay.
She had been wanting to change
her makeup lately anyway. Plus,
a new social group could make things
interesting. She had already made out
with most of the jocks at her school.
Betty's parents were not happy
with her transformation. Betty told
her parents she needed to express
her pain. "Why don't you express
your pain with a nice song and dance?"
Betty's father asked. "We could go buy you
some new tap shoes right now!"
her mother offered cheerfully.
Betty wasn't having it.
She threw a black hoodie
over her corset dress and slammed
the front door as she left the house.

By the time Betty was a junior
her parents had almost made peace
with her darker side.
But they did little to mask
their excitement the day Betty shimmied
into the kitchen wearing red lipstick and a polka-
dotted mini, asking for a grand
piano and a Victoria's Secret Angel Credit Card.

Visiting Family, Less-Than-Sexy Holiday

Your mother points out the spot where the denim
is wearing
away on the crotch of your father's jeans.
*That's great
for you, Mom*, you congratulate her.

The family dog gets to eat torn-up pancakes.

Your brother, who now speaks four languages,
repeats,
I grew up in your shadow.

You wonder how long you should use the
treadmill
after eating an entire gingerbread house.

You cannot tell the twin boy babies apart and you
don't care.

You make cherry turnovers.

You imagine yourself in a hot tub with three
of your ex-boyfriends.

Your cousin has her wiener dog model his entire
    wardrobe.

Snow.

You stand outside on a hill until your cold face
hurts.

You look like a movie star, your grandmother says.

You haven't had sex in five months.

The tree is still magic.

M as Herself as M
on Andy Warhol's "Marilyn x 100"

1

To play yourself
frozen in time.
To play yourself,
which plays her.
She must not move
a curl from the last time.
This hip must roll
again, like O, never thrust
like a V. Kisses must not
wilt while years of skin
cells shed like snow.

2

A naked body
wet with ink stains
and champagne spills
approaches a crisp
white sheet. The doors
are locked but the windows
are open. The stationary
is blank but the phone
is ringing.

The Male Torso

on Constantin Brancusi's "Male Torso"

The male torso will not budge an inch
unless it's toward the light and it's a light
that plays well upon the male torso.
Are you seeing this? asks the male torso.
Yes, I say, trying to sound annoyed
as I sneak a peek, the light playing up
the bronze of the male torso. A firm
and glistening pest, the male torso.

Repercussions of Glitter

I can't say I'm surprised. A part
of me always knew I'd end up
flat on my back in a muddy forest,
clad only in Oksana Bauil's fuzzy
pink skating costume from the
'94 Olympics. Didn't you know?
I missed my call time at the theater.
The dressing room, the make-up,
even the wings told me to get lost.
I spit on a piece of lighting equipment
and clicked off. Imagine my surprise,
ending up at Super Walmart, breaking
kitchen appliances. Snap snap like
my injured body. I could taste the
thuds, candy-sweet and metallic.
Like malt powder that's also dirt.

My Ex-Boyfriend Mitch
(Performed as Variations)

Variation 83

I dated Mitch when I was 19.

    I've never smoked a cigarette.

        Mitch cried when I broke up

            with him in my stairwell.

                He was adamant

that I keep his sweatpants.

Variation 5

I met my ex-boyfriend Mitch at a party.

    He wouldn't talk to me, but took several

pictures of me before passing out.

        Then I made out with his

    southern roommate John who called me

"baby doll."

Variation 25

If I were a lesbian, I could be on a free vacation

    with a Shakira look-a-like right now.

    I told some of my teenage dance students

    about the Shakira look-a-like.

        In the dressing room, they asked

    if I ever had considered becoming a lesbian.

        It's hard to lie to people

who have just watched you adjust
   your breasts in a push-up bra.

Variation Megg Dogg

My ex-boyfriend Mitch would wear his White Sox
   t-shirts in Wrigleyville.
        Mitch was three years older than me
   and thought it was a big age difference.
        I strongly disagreed.
                Mitch and I watched
      three men wearing speedos
      carry watermelons down Belmont.
                      It was a humid

summer night.

Variation Meglita Reversed

I'm currently a 20-something aspiring
   Mrs. Robinson.
        Intensely sexually attracted to a 19-year-old
           ballet dancer who has Asperger's
      syndrome and lives with his parents.
           My friend Stacy shamed me.
                   My friend Elizabeth said
      I should write about the time I was in a
                   neck brace, yelling at the
      delivery guy from Pizza Extreme.

Variation Toledo Boy

Mitch introduced me to his mother over dinner.
That's when I also met his mother's
lesbian life partner, Kathy.

Kathy was Mitch's fourth grade
teacher.

Mitch's mom and Kathy
had a sperm donor baby named Charlotte.
At dinner, there
was another suburban lesbian couple.
The brunette was named
Maureen and the blond
drove the mini-van that
we all rode in after dinner.

Variation My Metaphorical Penis Swings Wildly
My ex-boyfriend Mitch was furious when I gave
my number to another man.

I was 19 and seeing what I could get away
with.

Mitch said "I'm afraid" when
someone knocked on my door around 3 a.m.
Mitch stayed in bed as I
tiptoed quietly towards the door.

Variation 39078058162661
My ex-boyfriend Mitch would wear torn-up jeans
with plaid pajama bottoms underneath.
My ex-boyfriend Mitch took me

to the Lincoln Park Zoo
the day after we had sex for the first time.

My ex-boyfriend Mitch started
doing 10 sit-ups a day after I agreed to go out
with him.

I guess he meant to flatter me by
telling me about it.

Variation Now What?
Meg is short for Margaret.

Calling me Megan is like kidnapping
my mother and forcing her to live in a shopping
mall for the rest of her life.

Variation Twizzler
Mitch would say to me, "You're the most beautiful
woman I've ever known in real life."

That wasn't his own line.

Chandler said it to Monica
on the show *Friends*.

Mitch and I attended an
arts school gone wild.

At parties, we
didn't buy Adderall without a prescription for
crazy energy.

But all of our friends did.

Variation That's Czech!

My ex-boyfriend Mitch had to borrow my tools.
    I yelled at him for not having any of his own.
        My ex-boyfriend Mitch got drunk
on Manhattans.

        Then told me he didn't
like my hair in a bun.

Variation Hezka Holka

I always knew there would be many much-older
    men in my future.
        I didn't know how many of these men
    would have erectile dysfunction.

Variation Fast Walker

My ex-boyfriend Mitch owned two bath towels.
        My ex-boyfriend Mitch bought me a box
of Life cereal.

        He was beaming with pride.

Variation Garbo Lite

Having a Gemini Barbie in my apartment does not
    mean I still play with dolls.
        Got that, Luella?
        She's still in the box, for heaven's
sake!

        She watches over me like
a bedazzled brunette doll angel.

Variation 1920

My ex-boyfriend Mitch would chain-smoke Camel
   Lights.

      I'll always love Camel Lights via
   secondhand smoke.

A line on my boyfriend's
forehead runs diagonally
as if one side of his face
has accepted aging more
than the other.

Some days he seems
a man who has declared
war on himself. The spiral
staircase in his loft looks
ready to collapse from
his weight.

Other days he calls from his
office to ask me if I'm okay
with the current temperature
of his apartment. The staircase
looks larger.

*I don't mean to be ferocious with
you. I'm mad at myself*, he says.
Spinning in a desk chair at 2 am,
grunge rock through ear
phones as he sleeps, meanwhile
I seem to be getting younger.

She Ruins Her Hair, Plays House

She was in his kitchen, eating a third banana,
    and drinking
a fourth glass of water. Recovering from her
    simultaneous orgasm
and leg cramp. He was already asleep.

Sometimes when she was alone in his house,
    or when he was
asleep, she would pretend it was her house.

It was by the woods. When she looked out the
    back window
she imagined wolves moving closer to her in the
    dark.

She should have felt sorry for him. His bad back,
    his bad
performance. But she didn't. And on top of that,
    she had
dyed her hair red just to make him angry.

Who would she date next?

She felt the cold machinery of her body. An alarm

   that would go
off when jostled.

She knew some things were mostly for decorative
   purposes.

She could feel it: her body
like a weathervane.

Seeing My Boyfriend's Mother in a Swimsuit for the First Time

is plastic red sledding
down the iciest hill. Is
homemade slip 'n slide
made from black trash
bags, sprinkler and hose
water, grass crashes.
Floral clad pelvis
from which came his pelvis.
In Limon dance technique,
they scream *running pelvis*
which means *glide*,
but I was seventeen then
and thinking of an army
of asexual bones coming
at me. I'm far from seventeen
now, and still don't know
much about fake gliding.

I have so many questions about the world.
Why do I only see ugly people reading
The New Yorker? Did Jesus really happen?
Has there ever been a book called *Showering
with Jesus*? Someone look that up for me.
I'm too tired from being stalked by lesbian
bartenders. Sometimes lesbian bartenders
look at me with hungry eyes. Do they think I
taste like potato chips? Lots of people have
PhDs, but none of them can tell me what
Shakespeare's writing process was like. Screw
higher education. I'm gonna have a séance.

You Should Know

I do not like being lumped
together with these Fudgsicles.

I am very haughty for a dented
can of pineapple.

Whatever.

We'll see who the champ is
when the power goes out.

M Divided

We've lost track
of her, but she always
comes back. Her lips
bucking up, accepting
more lipstick. I say
her eyes are too sad,
you tell me to sit
down for dinner. But
I know what it's like
to have too many
selves, I want to say.
To feel my future ghost,
its gray parts mingling
with my pinkness. You
tell me we'll be late for
the movie. That you
don't know if I'm a lamb
or a lioness, sugar
or kerosene.

Pretending to Read *Time Magazine*

1

in an agency waiting room
with an article about politics
I was actually reading it
until the tornado sirens
started blasting their hum
I'm in white knee high tube socks
with black rings at the top
attempting to look "young
& funky" for my three minute audition
a four hour commute for three minutes
but I can't find anything better to do
I'm a baby face, but I'm a wild card
don't you know I'm 26 years old now?
I want to shout above the sirens
I'm finally seen, then out the door
into a pretty landscape
but I know rebellion
even under popsicle hues

2

stomping around
piles of clothes
on my floor

in a see-through white tank
& lacy pink boy shorts
pop music is swarming around my body
but I'm still haunted
by Adrienne Rich & her *Time is male*
and in his cups drinks to the fair.
I'm thinking about bouncing little
girls, elderly ladies with glossy
smiles, all of them lovely
all seemingly content
calm & quiet, their contained power
. . . . *Time is male*
I pace against these words
as if walking around at home in my
underwear could truly make a difference

Bad Girls

As much as I would like to
validate my troubles by calling
them rebellious, I might just be
another twenty-something artist.

I think myself the naughty
rebel-girl but how do I
compare to girls gone wild, actual
naughty schoolgirls?

Loads of debt, a forthcoming
I-masturbate-to-porn poem,
a masochistic need to be
a performer, sleeping with an older
divorced man, and returning to
college after dropping out.

Really, how edgy can my
I-don't-like-to-clean-my-room
attitude be?

I tried being a hipster for indie
appeal but it just wouldn't stick. I
need to be within reaching distance

of a hairbrush twenty-four hours a
day or else I get anxious.

I only pretend to be one now
when I want
someone to lie in the grass with me.
I look great in the grass. Yeah...

What stance should I take to end this?
How much of a bad girl am I?
Is there a measuring system?

I just turned twenty-seven. I have
dark brown Marcia-Brady-hair.

2010 was like a girl named Brittany
making fun of the name Tiffany.
There were too many pictures of
babies on Facebook. One baby
was wearing a onesie that read
I'm with the band. If the newborn
could talk, it would have said, *Mom,*
you're in a local Celtic music group.
Get me out of this retarded outfit.
I'm not any better. Last year, my idea
of a high tech science experiment
was putting hydrogen peroxide
on my hair to see if it would:

A) lighten
B) fall out
C) both
D) none of the above

You may have noticed that I like
to make jokes. I do. But some things
are truly too terrible to joke about.
Like having to spend an evening with
Marshall Scholars. I had to liven up that

reception by standing on a table
and proclaiming *I don't care
what anyone says. I still like
Jennifer Lopez.* After carrying me out
of the banquet room, my boyfriend
asked me why I did that. *Cause I'm real,*
I said. I was kind of hoping people
would call me M. Jo after that,
but it never happened.

Sex Brain

I can hear the alphabet, the letters
clanking on the sidewalk, falling
out of my head/brain/head. My
noggin is surfing on bodies, body
surfing, body heat/hot. I want
to tell you about the crime, how
the factories make the whole city
smell like burning plastic or an
animal hospital. Something
apocalyptic. But I can't remember.
My body is a harmonica, any
improvisation will work, any
scenario involving a man sitting
on a porch will do. At least as a start.
Press start.

We are pre-code Hollywood,
sweating bourbon and champagne.
We are black and white pixel
ladies, holding a kiss behind
big hats. We will not keep one foot
on the floor as we tumble to the bed.
Our fingerprints reveal multiple
unnecessary undressing scenes.
We are strong female leads,
our expiration date pinned
in our hair with diamond
barrettes. Blaring trumpets sound
like thigh high stockings as we lean
against jail bars. We stand behind
our matching podiums blindfolded.
We're gentlemen in tuxedos waltzing
in a boxing ring.
                    Ding.

These Waves Are Mine

on Paul Gauguin's "In the Waves"

Leaving a breathing body
of clothing waiting for me
on the shore, I had never
before let outdoor air greet
my spine. Whispering currents
ushered in a shoulder. Icy
thighs, throat open, roaming
forward. Wading through
a buzzing green orchestra.

I found a lady in the grass. Lying
parallel to the trash cans. Someone
thought the row of grey plastic
was enough of a shield. A hiding
place. I had never seen someone who
looked like the Venus paintings before.
And I had never before seen Venus
clutching a purse, its empty pockets
turned inside out.

One Working Headlight

One working headlight won't look you in the face. One working headlight shines on your shoulders and thighs. One working headlight writes the ransom note after the murder. *There is no broken headlight* says the one working headlight. One working headlight has cinnamon and pliers, rubies and cowboy hats. One working headlight says to meet it at the train station at 5 am. It doesn't show up. You drag your duffel bag along the sidewalk as you walk home.

The Lovers Manual and Dating Guide (2012)*

with New Rules for Urban Living!

Worst foods to eat off your lover's naked body:

1. Chex Mix
2. Caesar Salad
3. Cottage Cheese
4. A Pork Chop

Worst pick-up lines:
1. How do *you* feel about the Mayan calendar?
2. I'm a Newt Gingrich type looking for my Callista…
3. I miss Y2K.
4. I could get you so wet, you'd have to blow dry your hair afterward.

Worst bedroom role playing scenarios:
1. Justin Bieber paternity scandal
2. Jimmy John's employee and customer
3. Two unemployed people
4. Mary Magdalene and Jesus

New trends in romantic getaways on a budget:
1. Eating Taco Bell in a forest

2.   Wearing beach-wear at the public library
3.   Speaking in fake French accents at a park
4.   Reading a history book in the shower

Newest ways to deal with a lovers' spat:
1.   Distract your lover with a piñata
2.   Sort it out by leg wrestling
3.   Write about your feelings with Elmer's
   glue on a table top
4.   Play a five hour game of Uno

Best new tips for urban living:
1.   Never give your younger lover a lunchable.
Even if your younger lover really wants one. If you
must present your younger lover with a lunchable
it must not be in public. Close all the blinds. Make
sure they drink the Capri Sun. It has Vitamin C.
2.   Never assume you are the Vince in your
Entourage sized group of friends. See your friend
with the slightly darker and shinier hair. Yep.
3.   Don't ask your neighbor for a cup of
sugar.

I Don't Feel Well

I should have never consumed
that canned spray cheese or
celebrity poetry. It's all sold
in bulk though nobody ever ordered it.
I'm hiding under the bed from
child beauty pageant shows.
I've cleared space in the basement
to protect myself from
tornadoes and scientology.
If you think I sound like an ass
I'll point my toes and show you
I'm pretty. If you howl at the moon
I won't tell anyone.

Something like an Artist

I wasn't born to admire seashells.

If a British theater director with
bad teeth comes to America and
demands to see an American
dentist, I'm going to get suspicious.

I'm not a fan of the phrase *life changing*.

I like to drink cold water.

I stopped wearing a side ponytail.

Dear God. How will they sell me
without a ponytail?

Thighs equal side ponytail.
Voice equals side ponytail.
Blinking equals side ponytail.
Five years side ponytail.
Buy me a steak and have sex
with me side ponytail.

Now people say: *She is channeling*

her inner Pina Bausch.

I would love to talk Pina Baucsh.

But first I want to listen to this
T-Pain song. (Because I've been
so Chopped N Screwed.)

The real victim in my life is my
housemate who, in public, has to
act like I am a very sophisticated
person who does not(!) listen
to T-Pain songs.

Being in this Gymboree class
makes me feel dirty.

I wanna tell you something
about me and some strangers.

There comes a moment in every young
woman's life when she must tear herself
away from the Cocoa Krispies long enough
to say to the world:

*I no longer wish to be in an exclusive
relationship with a college basketball coach.*

*I want to have sex with a man wearing
bubble wrap.*

Donkey Day

The worst phrase ever uttered:
The piñata is only for the kids.
My professor boyfriend has
taken me to a garden party. It turns
out to be a surprise wedding. I
wish this meant people would
stop saying *garden party,* but
they don't. I stare at the piñata
sulking. Later, I take a picture
of the decapitated rainbow
donkey body and one of a little
girl with a bob wearing the broken
off head as a hat. My boyfriend
excitedly talks to former students.
I scarf down another cupcake.

Traveling Woman

I'm driving a riding lawn mower
and wearing a pink tiara. I'm not doing it
to be sexy. I'm in a hurry. Please go
back to pretending to read books. Or
you could clean out your car, take all
the jock straps to Goodwill. By the time
you finish that I'll be in Nebraska,
going through a McDonald's drive
through. When the polite red sky tells
me it will be dark soon, I will stop to
rest and duct tape my heart down
from beating in your direction.

Kept Woman

I am my own woman. I keep
myself in a hat box. Not even my
lover knows where I live. It's glam.
It's painful. I don't know how to
stop. When I powder my nose,
I can't see anything and my hair
ends up powdered-sugar white.
Sometimes I'll go for a walk.
It sure feels good to stretch
the legs, but I always know the hat
box is waiting. Waiting
to see how I'll shut myself in this time.

When I took a break
from dance, I retrieved
pairs of pointe shoes
from the company shelves.
They were missing
the elastic bands and ribbons
I had sewn on. I could
guess which vulture
had trespassed. *Pointe
shoe graveyard*, I thought
as I stuffed them into
my bag, imagining her,
after I left, pulling the piece
of masking tape with my name
off the shelves and
flushing it down the toilet.

Here, but not Easily Seen

Somewhere between the *I*
was a stripper, now I'm
not a stripper narratives
and the scholars so scholarly
they always wear underwear,
I am tucked in like your
grandmother's 1920's
lace valentines. Please dig
for me. Your fingers may
cramp, but that's not what
you'll remember.

The Odd Couple Remake

I'm an Oscar, not a Felix.
You can find where I am in
the apartment by the trail of
empty pop cans. My boyfriend
suggests we host his co-worker's
baby shower and I raise my eyebrows
like Walter Matthau, scrunching my
forehead into disapproving lined
sections. I have a laundry pile knee
high, mostly of deceptively girly
lace thongs. My boyfriend's
t-shirts hang on white hangers,
color coded. Who knows... If he
wasn't putting out regularly, I
might throw his frittata against
a kitchen wall.

One Lie, Zero Questions

I'm in a windowless room with a woman
who lies about her age. *They told me
to do it*, she coos. She starts dancing
as if there is music playing like some
sort of possessed Lolita doll. She's
older than me and an actress, but I
feel like a volunteer mentor at a middle
school. She pauses from her watered down
hip hop moves. *You have to protect me,
I'm a girlie girl*, she says, even though
she is a grown woman and I am slighter
than her. She is a stereotype—
rainbow sprinkles and soft-core porn.
I command her to dump out the contents
of her oversized purse, in case there is
something in there that can help us.
She looks at me with wide eyes after
her tiny objects have scattered across
the floor. I've never heard her ask a
question. I pull a flask out of my own
purse and sigh.

How long is too long
to ride on this elephant
for you? I'm starting
to feel ridiculous up here,
the two piece sequined
bathing suit and the feather
headdress. You gesture
for another loop around
the tent. The audience
murmurs. *I can help you
down from there, sweetheart,*
a man yells out somewhere
in the crowd. *I'll take you
someplace real nice.*
The make-up on my face
is dry and cracking. My smile
is cracking. My inner
thighs are cracking. You don't
seem to hear the crowd's
disapproval. Or maybe you do,
your face stern under your
jaunty hat. Backstage, I know
the trapeze duo is warming up.
I wonder if it's too late
to take up the trapeze.

The Guest

Nothing says *you're not*
getting married more
than someone else's wedding
dress hanging up in your
bedroom. Its beady-eyed
row of buttons look
your body up and down.
Don't spill anything
on that, your boyfriend-
best-friend-of-the-groom
jokes. Laugh.

What You're Looking For

…If you're lookin' for trouble, just look right in my face.
I was born standin' up…

My onesie didn't have to have
evil scrawled across its chest,
my parents knew to dress me
as the devil. *That's right,*
make me a tin foil pitch fork.

If Lolitas don't die they become
Cougars. If Cougars are animals
then animals run the world. If
the world is a foxtrot can I get
a refund? And a redo?

Let me tell you what *Reduce,*
Reuse, Recycle means. It means
running out of boyfriends.
Dating four guys named Chris.
I called the last one Joe.

Let's get this ménage a trois started.
You, me, and this three legged
dog of a city. The most majestic
creature here is a blimp in the sky,
soaring over abandoned warehouses.
Middle class looking houses are
undercover brothels. Drive through
convenience stores face vandalized
elementary schools.

Let's pretend gas stations are romantic.
My house by the highway could
be a lovers' paradise if we get naked fast
enough. When your body outshines
my past lovers and this city, I
won't know if I'm happy or sad.

Acknowledgments

Thank you to the following publications, where poems from this manuscript originally appeared:

Atticus Review: "The Guest" and "One Lie, Zero Questions"
The Battered Suitcase: "Bad Girls" and "You Should Know"
Camroc Press Review: ""Be Prepared,"" "I Should Be in Jail,"
and "Practice"
Clutching at Straws: "I Don't Get It"
Counterexample Poetics: "The Male Torso," "No Code," "One
Working Headlight," and "These Waves are Mine"
The Destroyer: "Sex Brain"
Gesture Zine: "44306"
The Jet Fuel Review: "Fascinatin' Rhythm," "The Girl," and
"Repercussions of Glitter"
Left Behind: A Journal of Shock Literature: "A Green Dress"
Midwestern Gothic: "Traveling Woman"
Punchnel's: "Donkey Day" and "Here, but not Easily Seen"
Pure Francis: "Welcome, Welcome, 2011"
Radioactive Moat: "Pretending to Read Time Magazine"
Red Moon District: Underground Voices Anthology: "The Odd
Couple Remake"
Rufous City Review: "What You're Looking For"
Slipstream Magazine: "My Ex-Boyfriend Mitch (Performed as
Variations)"

Slurve Magazine: "I Don't Feel Well" and "The Lovers
Manual and Dating Guide (2012)"
Smoking Glue Gun: "Showgirl"
SOFTBLOW: "Live-In," "M as Herself as M," "M
Divided," and "Seeing My Boyfriend's Mother in a Swimsuit for
the First Time"
Stone Highway Review: "Lady in the Grass" and "Rival"
U.S. 1 Worksheets: "Betty Boop Goes Goth"
The Waterhouse Review: "Kept Woman"
Word Riot: "Timber!"
WTF PWM: "Something like an Artist" and "The
Unfortunate Charisma"
Yahara Journal: "She Ruins Her Hair, Plays House" and
"Visiting Family, Less-Than-Sexy Holiday"

"My Ex-Boyfriend Mitch (Performed as Variations)" was
reprinted in *Asinine Poetry*
"The Unfortunate Charisma" was reprinted in *Midwestern
Gothic*

Also from The National Poetry Review Press

Lucktown by Bryan Penberthy

Bill's Formal Complaint by Dan Kaplan

Gilgamesh at the Bellagio by Karl Elder

Legend of the Recent Past by James Haug

Urchin to Follow by Dorine Jennette

The Kissing Party by Sarah E. Barber

Deepening Groove by Ravi Shankar

The City from Nome by James Grinwis

Fort Gorgeous by Angela Vogel

Able, Baker, Charlie by John Mann

The Wanted by Michael Tyrell

Loud Dreaming in a Quiet Room by Betsy Wheeler

Guest Host by Elizabeth Hughey

Manual for Extinction by Caroline Manring

Inside the Color of Water by Lynne Potts

Please visit our website for more information:

www.nationalpoetryreview.com